Other giftbooks by Helen Exley:
Golf...A Good Walk Spoiled   Golf Quotations
A Round of Golf Jokes   Golf Score Book

Published simultaneously in 1997 by Exley Giftbooks in the USA and Exley Publications Ltd in Great Britain.

12 11 10 9 8 7 6 5 4 3

Border illustrations by Judith O'Dwyer
Copyright © Helen Exley 1997.
The moral right of the author has been asserted.
Edited and pictures selected by Helen Exley.

A HELEN EXLEY GIFTBOOK.

ISBN 1-85015-929-7

Exley Publications Ltd, 16 Chalk Hill, Watford, Herts WD1 4BN, UK.
Exley Publications LLC, 232 Madison Avenue, Suite 1409, NY 10016, USA.

Pictures researched by Image Select International.
Typeset by Delta, Watford.
Printed and bound in China.

Acknowledgements: The publishers are grateful for permission to reproduce copyright material. Whilst every effort has been made to trace copyright holders, the publishers wou be pleased to hear from any not here acknowledged. HENRY BEARD AND ROY MCKIE: Extracts from *Golfing - A Duffer's Dictionary* by Henry Beard and Roy Mckie, published by Methuen, London; TOM O'CONNOR: Extracts from *One Flew Over the Clubhouse* by Tom O'Connor, published by Robson Books Ltd., reprinted with permission of Robson Books L MIKE SEABROOK: Extracts from *One Over Par* by Peter Alliss and Mike Seabrook, published by H. F. and G. Witherby Ltd., a division of Cassell; Extracts from *Golf Forever, Work Whenever,* compiled by Michael Ryan, © 1993 by The Great Quotations Company.
Picture credits: Exley Publications is very grateful to the following individuals and organizations for permission to reproduce their pictures: © 1997 Sarah Fabian Baddiel, Golfiania, Grays in the Mews, B10 Davies Mews, London W1, tel: 0171-408-1239.

GOLF
Quips

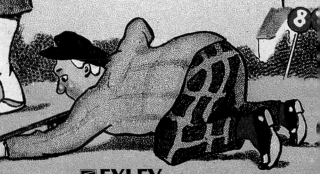

≡ EXLEY
NEW YORK • WATFORD, UK

GOLF:
A game in which you claim
the privileges of age, and retain
the playthings of childhood.

SAMUEL JOHNSON

GOLF:
A day spent in a round
of strenuous idleness.

WILLIAM WORDSWORTH

I regard golf as an expensive way
of playing marbles.

G.K. CHESTERTON

In primitive societies they call it witchcraft
when the local tribes beat the ground with
clubs. In civilised society it's called golf.

O. CUPIDO

If you watch a game, it's fun.
If you play it, it's recreation.
If you work at it, it's golf.

BOB HOPE

Golf is a good walked spoiled.

MARK TWAIN

Golfball: a sphere made of rubber bands wound up about half as tensely as the man trying to hit it.

ANONYMOUS

Green: An area of smooth grass with a hole in the bumpy bit.

PETER GAMMOND,
from *"Bluff Your Way In Golf"*

Willis' Rule of Golf:
You can't lose an old golf ball.

JOHN WILLIS

Handicap: an allocation of strokes on one or more holes that permits two golfers of very different ability to do equally poorly on the same course.

HENRY BEARD
AND ROY MCKIE

Hole in-one: an occurrence in which a ball is hit directly from the tee into the hole on a single shot by a golfer playing alone.

HENRY BEARD
AND ROY MCKIE

Golf is the only game that pits
the player against an opponent,
the weather, the minutest details of a large
chunk of local topography and his own
nervous system, all at the same time.

MIKE SEABROOK,
from *"One Over Par"*

I have only one goal in golf –
to leave it with my sanity.

JOE INMAN

Real golfers go to work to relax.

GEORGE DILLON

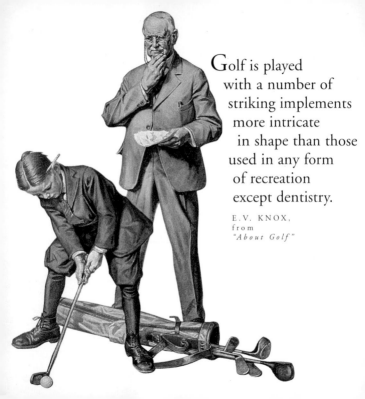

Golf is played
with a number of
striking implements
more intricate
in shape than those
used in any form
of recreation
except dentistry.

E.V. KNOX,
from
"About Golf"

The trouble that most of us find
with the modern matched sets of clubs
is that they don't really seem to know
any more about the game
than the old one's did!

ROBERT BROWNING,
from
"A History Of Golf"

Golf is a game whose aim is to hit
a very small ball into an even
smaller hole, with weapons singularly
ill-designed for the purpose.

SIR WINSTON CHURCHILL

No matter what calamities befall him
in everyday life, the true hacker
still needs the pressure and inconvenience
of four hours of trudging in wind or rain
or sleet or sun (or all of them at once),
hacking at a white pellet that seems
to have a mind of its own, and
a lousy sense of direction.

TOM O'CONNOR,
from
"One Flew Over The Clubhouse"

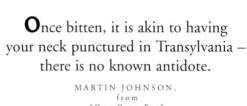

Once bitten, it is akin to having
your neck punctured in Transylvania –
there is no known antidote.

MARTIN JOHNSON,
from
"One Over Par"

"After all, golf is only a game",
said Millicent. Women say these things
without thinking. It does not mean that
there is any kink in their character.
They simply don't realise what they
are saying.

P.G. WODEHOUSE

*Golf is like a love affair. If you don't take it
too seriously, it's no fun; if you do take it
seriously, it breaks your heart.*

ARNOLD DALY

If the rest of his foursome are bunched directly behind his ball, or assume the foetal position with their backs to the tee, the Golfer is reminded that his drive tends to be erratic. More cruel yet is for his opponent to stand directly in the projected line of flight, as the safest place to be.

ERIC NICOL AND DAVE MORE,
from
*"Golf. The Agony
And The Ecstasy"*

The actual distance a bad golfer
is going to hit a ball with any club
obviously depends on many factors,
not the least of which is whether the ball
was actually hit at all.

LESLIE NIELSON AND HENRY BEARD,
from
"Bad Golf My Way"

If it goes right, it's a slice.
If it goes left, it's a hook.
If it goes straight, it's a miracle.

T-SHIRT

I find it more satisfying to be
a bad player at golf. The worse you play,
the better you remember the occasional
good shot.

NUBAR GULBENKIAN

"*Daddy,*"
said the bright child,
accompanying her father
on a round of golf,
"*why mustn't the ball*
go in the hole?"

ANONYMOUS

The most exquisitely satisfying act in the world of golf is that of throwing a club. The full backswing, the delayed wrist action, the flowing follow-through, followed by that unique whirring sound, reminiscent only of a passing flock of starlings, are without parallel in sport.

HENRY LONGHURST

I've thrown or broken
a few clubs
in my day. In fact,
I guess
at one time or another
I probably held
distance records
for every club
in the bag.

TOMMY BOLT,
from
*"How To Keep
Your Temper On
The Golf Course"*

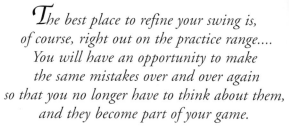

The best place to refine your swing is, of course, right out on the practice range.... You will have an opportunity to make the same mistakes over and over again so that you no longer have to think about them, and they become part of your game.

STEPHEN BAKER,
from
"How To Play Golf In The Low 120's"

There is no movement in the golf swing so difficult that it cannot be made even more difficult by careful study and difficult practice.

from *"Golf Forever, Work Whenever"*,
COMP. MICHAEL RYAN

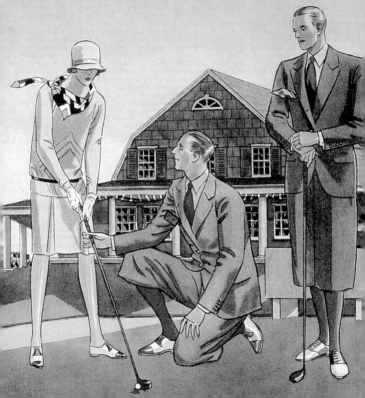

*... the course designers and the pros
are in collusion.
One is paid to drive you mad
by making the course impossible.
The other is paid to drive you mad
teaching you how to overcome
the obstacles that shouldn't have been
there in the first place.*

HELEN RICHARDS

Practice Tee: The place where golfers go
to convert a nasty hook into a wicked slice.

HENRY BEARD AND ROY MCKIE

Golf is essentially an exercise in masochism conducted out of doors.

PAUL O'NEIL

... humiliations are the essence of the game.

ALISTAIR COOKE

Like other forms of compulsive behavior, for true golfaholics even nine holes are more than they should attempt, yet 18 holes are not enough to satisfy their insatiable craving for humiliation and self-abuse.

MARK OMAN,
from
"Portrait Of A Golfaholic"

While it is true that some amateur golfers are unwittingly or unwillingly duped, badgered, or coerced into playing a round of golf, an incredible 97 per cent of the dummies actually report to the first tee on a *voluntary* basis.

GEOFF HOWSON,
from *"Golf: How To Look Good
When You're Not"*

A Coarse Golfer
is one who has to shout "Fore"
when he putts.

MICHAEL GREEN,
from
"The Art Of Coarse Golf"

"Well done Seve,
I knew if we kept at it
you'd hit a fairway."

SEVE BALLESTEROS
AND JOSE MARIA OLAZABAL,
on the 18th hole,
Ryder Cup 1991,
Kiawah Island.

You've just one problem.
You stand too close to
the ball – after you've hit it.

SAM SNEAD

The secret of missing a tree
is to aim straight at it.

MICHAEL GREEN,
from
"The Art Of Coarse Golf"

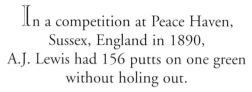

In a competition at Peace Haven, Sussex, England in 1890, A.J. Lewis had 156 putts on one green without holing out.

DONALD STEEL,
from
"The Guinness Book Of Golf Facts And Feats"

It took me seventeen years to get three thousand hits in baseball. I did it in one afternoon on the golf course.

HANK AARON

My golf is improving.
Yesterday I hit the ball in one!

JANE SWAN

If you are going to throw a club, it is important to throw it ahead of you, down the fairway, so you don't waste energy going back to pick it up.

TOMMY BOLT

Golfer Tommy Bolt
is known for his sweet swing and
foul temper. While giving a clinic
to a group of amateurs,
Bolt tried to show his softer side
by involving his fourteen-year-old son
in the lesson. "Show the nice folks
what I taught you," said Bolt.
His son obediently took a nine iron,
cursed, and hurled it into the sky.

THOMAS BOSWELL

Golf acts as a corrective against sinful pride. I attribute the insane arrogance of the later Roman emperors almost entirely to the fact that, never having played golf, they never knew that strange chastening humility which is engendered by a topped chip shot. If Cleopatra had been ousted in the first round of the Ladies' Singles, we should have heard a lot less of her proud imperiousness.

P.G. WODEHOUSE

Many a golfer prefers a golf cart
to a caddy because it cannot count,
criticize or laugh.

from
"Golf Forever, Work Whenever",
COMP. MICHAEL RYAN

I was lying ten and had a thirty-five-foot
putt. I whispered over my shoulder:
"How does this one break?"
And my caddie said, "Who cares?"

JACK LEMMON

GOLFER:
You must be the worst caddie
in the world.
CADDIE:
No sir, we couldn't 'ave a coincidence
like that.

HENRY LONGHURST

LANCE THACKERAY

GOLFER:
You perhaps won't believe it,
but I once did this hole
in one.
CADDIE:
Stroke or day, Sir?

KEN DODD

GOLFER:
I've never played
this poorly before.
CADDIE:
You've played before?

FRED METCALF

After each hole has been completed
the golfer counts his strokes.
Then he subtracts six and says,
"Made that in five. That's one above par.
Shall we play for fifty cents
on the next hole, too, Ed?"

from *"Golf Digest"*

Golf appeals to the idiot in us and the child.
What child does not grasp the simple
pleasure-principle of miniature golf?
Just how childlike golf players become
is proved by their frequent inability
to count past five.

JOHN UPDIKE

The difference between a sand trap
and water is the difference between a car
crash and an airplane crash.
You have a chance of recovering from
a car crash.

BOBBY JONES

The object of a bunker or trap
is not only to punish a physical mistake,
to punish lack of control, but also
to punish pride and egotism.

CHARLES BLAIR MACDONALD

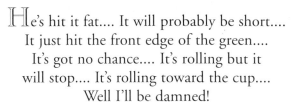

He's hit it fat.... It will probably be short....
It just hit the front edge of the green....
It's got no chance.... It's rolling but it
will stop.... It's rolling toward the cup....
Well I'll be damned!

JIMMY DEMARET

Watching The Masters on CBS is like
attending a church service.
Announcers speak in hushed, pious tones,
as if to convince us that something of great
meaning and historical importance is
taking place. What we are actually seeing
is grown men hitting little balls
with sticks.

TOM GILMORE

ANNOUNCER:
This is the big one, folks....
Now he's sighting the putt.... Now he's
bending over and addressing the ball....
Now he's glaring in my direction.

ROBERT DAY,
a cartoon in *"The New Yorker"*

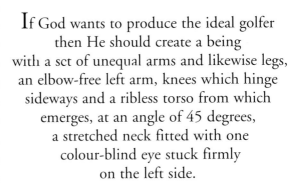

If God wants to produce the ideal golfer
then He should create a being
with a set of unequal arms and likewise legs,
an elbow-free left arm, knees which hinge
sideways and a ribless torso from which
emerges, at an angle of 45 degrees,
a stretched neck fitted with one
colour-blind eye stuck firmly
on the left side.

CHRIS PLUMRIDGE,
from
"Almost Straight Down The Middle"

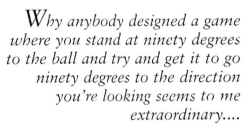

*W*hy anybody designed a game
where you stand at ninety degrees
to the ball and try and get it to go
ninety degrees to the direction
you're looking seems to me
extraordinary....

H.R.H. THE DUKE OF YORK

Golf is a terrible, hopeless addiction,
it seems: it makes its devotees willing
to trudge miles in any manner of weather,
lugging a huge, incommodious and
appallingly heavy bag with them, in pursuit
of a tiny and fantastically expensive ball,
in a fanatical attempt to direct it into a hole
the size of a beer glass half a mile away.
If anything could be better calculated
to convince one of the essential lunacy
of the human race, I haven't found it.

MIKE SEABROOK,
from *"One Over Par"*

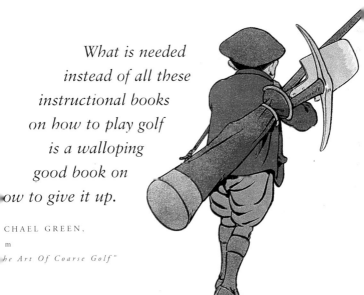

What is needed instead of all these instructional books on how to play golf is a walloping good book on ow to give it up.

CHAEL GREEN,
m
he Art Of Coarse Golf"

*T*o the comedian, George Burns:
"George, you look perfect... that beautiful
knitted shirt, an alpaca sweater,
those expensive slacks.... You've got
an alligator bag, the finest matched irons, and
the best woods money can buy.
It's a damned shame you have to spoil it
all by playing golf."

LLOYD MANGRUN

I'd give up golf if I didn't have
so many sweaters.

BOB HOPE

When
you get up there
in years,
the fairways
get longer
and the holes
get smaller.

BOBBY LOCKE

Playing [golf] and breathing air
in spite of an increasing girth,
poor eyesight, dicky heart, varicose veins
and blood pressure is a defiant gesture
by those whose lives are otherwise
devoted to concentrated dissipation
and indulgence.

PETER GAMMOND,
from
"*Bluff Your Way In Golf*"

If only I had taken up golf earlier
and devoted my whole life to it
instead of fooling about writing stories
and things, I might have got my handicap
down to under eighteen.

P.G. WODEHOUSE

Golf is probably the only known game
a man can play as long as a quarter of
a century and then discover
it was too deep for him in the first place.

SEYMOUR DUNN,
from
"The Complete Golf Joke Book"

$\mathcal{B}$ob Hope tells the story that his doctor
told him he was overworked for a man
in his eighties and needed a complete rest –
and that included giving up golf.
Hope decided to give up his doctor
instead.

BOB MONKHOUSE

I'll go on living as long as I can.
I've got a few jokes for the box.
If they raise the lid I'll say a few words
on the way to the last hole.

BOB HOPE

After the final,
or eighteenth hole,
the golfer adds up his score
and stops when he has reached
eighty-seven.
He then has a swim,
a pint of rye,
sings "Sweet Adelinc"
with six or eight
other liars
and calls it the end
of a perfect day,

ANONYMOUS